ANIMAL KINGDOM CLASSIFICATION

ANGELFISH, MEGAMOUTH SHARKS & OTHER

FISH

By Steve Parker
Content Adviser: Debbie Folkerts, Ph.D., Assistant Professor
of Biological Sciences, Auburn University, Alabama

Science Adviser: Terrence E. Young Jr., M.Ed., M.L.S.,
Jefferson (Louisiana) Public School System

First published in the United States in 2006 by
Compass Point Books
3109 West 50th St., #115
Minneapolis, MN 55410

ANIMAL KINGDOM CLASSIFICATION–FISH
was produced by

David West Children's Books
7 Princeton Court
55 Felsham Road
London SW15 1AZ

Designer: David West
Editors: Nadia Higgins, Kate Newport
Page Production: Les Tranby, James Mackey

Visit Compass Point Books on the Internet at
www.compasspointbooks.com
or e-mail your request to
custserv@compasspointbooks.com

Library of Congress Cataloging-in-Publication Data
Parker, Steve.
  Angelfish, megamouth sharks, and other fish /
by Steve Parker.
      p. cm. — (Animal kingdom classification)
  Includes bibliographical references (p.   ) and index.
  ISBN 0-7565-1252-2 (hard cover)
  1. Fishes—Juvenile literature. I. Title. II. Series.
  QL617.2.P358 2005
  597—dc22
                          2005004612

PHOTO CREDITS :
Abbreviations: t-top, m-middle, b-bottom, r-right, l-left, c-center.

8b, Oxford Scientific Films; 8b inset, Briandon Cole/naturepl.com; 12b, Oxford Scientific Films; 13tr, John Cancalos/naturepl.com; 13b, Oxford Scientific Films; 14br, Jeff Rotman/naturepl.com; 17t, David Shale/naturepl.com; 17m, Jurgen Freund/naturepl.com; 17b, Alan Root/Oxford Scientific Films; 22b, Fabio Liverani/naturepl.com; 23tr inset, Niall Benuie/naturepl.com; 23tr & 23mr, Doug Perrine/naturepl.com; 23br, Tim MacMillan/John Downer pr/naturepl.com; 24l, NOAA; 24t, 25tl & 26b, Doug Perine/naturepl.com; 27br, Hermann Brehm/naturepl.com; 28b, Jurgen Freund/naturepl.com; 29tl, Doug Allan/naturepl.com; 29tr,David Shale/naturepl.com; 29bl, Alan James/naturepl.com; 29bm, Constantinos Petrinos/naturepl.com; 33br Tim MacMillan/John Downer pr/naturepl.com; 35tl & br, Oxford Scientific Films; 38tr, Michael Pitts/naturepl.com; 39t, Doug Perrine/naturepl.com; 39bl, Alan James/naturepl.com; 39br, Pete Oxford/naturepl.com; 40bl, Doc White/naturepl.com; 40-41, David Shale/naturepl.com; 41tl, naturepl.com; 41tr, Bruce Rasner/Rotman/naturepl.com; 41b, Oxford Scientific Films; 42b & 42tr, Jurgen Freund/naturepl.com; 45b, Digital Vision.

Front cover: Clown fish
Opposite: Stonefish

ANIMAL KINGDOM CLASSIFICATION

ANGELFISH, MEGAMOUTH SHARKS & OTHER

FISH

Steve Parker

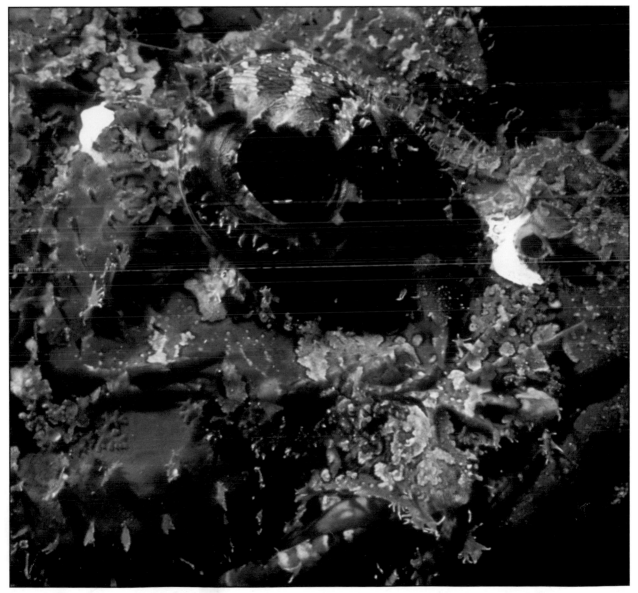

COMPASS POINT BOOKS ✦ MINNEAPOLIS, MINNESOTA

CONTENTS

INTRODUCTION 6

WATERY WORLDS 8

INSIDE A FISH 10

FISH THROUGH THE AGES 12

FINS, TAILS, AND SWIMMING 14

GILLS AND BREATHING 16

SKIN, SCALES, AND COLOR 18

FISHY SENSES 20

HOW FISH BREED 22

THE SHARK GROUP 24

"SNAKES OF THE SEA" 26

CATFISH, COD, AND ANGLERFISH 28

FLATTENED FISH 30

FISH OF LAKES AND RIVERS 32

SEASHORE FISH 34

THE COLORFUL REEF 36

OPEN OCEAN DWELLERS 38

FISH OF THE DEEP 40

FISH IN TROUBLE 42

ANIMAL CLASSIFICATION 44

ANIMAL PHYLA 45

GLOSSARY 46

FURTHER RESOURCES 47

INDEX 48

INTRODUCTION

Only a few fortunate people are able to visit the underwater world. They snorkel, scuba dive, or even ride in an underwater seacraft. This mysterious world is the home of fish—from tiny gobies and wrasse almost as small as these words, to huge sharks like the feared great white. Some say there are as many as 30,000 different species, or kinds, of fish—more than five times the number of mammals. They live in almost every body of water, from ditches and garden ponds to the wide-open ocean. They live under the polar ice caps and the deepest, darkest parts of the bottom of the sea.

Some types of fish are very familiar to us, especially those we keep as pets, such as goldfish, or those we like to eat. But other fish look strange or frightening and come from a world that is very different from our own on dry land. It can be difficult for us to appreciate how fish live their lives, sense their surroundings, find food, avoid enemies, and produce their young. This book dips beneath the water's surface to find out all of these facts, and more.

CRUISING GIANT

The biggest ray, and one of the largest of all fish, is the giant manta. Its winglike body can measure 23 feet (7 meters) across, and it can weigh up to 2 tons (1.8 metric tons). Usually it swims slowly, lazily flapping its "wings." But it can also leap out of water, crashing back in with a huge splash.

WATERY WORLDS

There are many different habitats on land, such as forests, grasslands, and deserts. Underwater, fish also live in a huge variety of habitats.

UNDERWATER VARIETY

There are as many habitats underwater as there are above. Polar seas where waves crash in great storms are very different from the warm, sheltered waters of a coral reef, the rushing torrent of a mountain stream, or the still, muddy water in a tropical swamp. Fish have adapted to all of these habitats, and more.

Fish habitats are divided into two main groups—salt water and fresh water. Most fish live either in salty ocean water or in the fresh water of ponds, lakes, and rivers. Only a few species can move between the two. Some, like salmon and eels, do so only at certain stages of their lives.

TWO KINDS OF CARTILAGINOUS FISH
Sharks like the reef shark (main picture) and rays such as the eagle ray (left) are the two main kinds of fish with skeletons made of cartilage.

JAWLESS AND SLIMY

Lampreys and hagfish have no jaws, just like the first fish on Earth. The mouth is just a rounded opening with small "teeth" used for scraping food. Lampreys have seven pairs of rounded gill openings behind the eyes, no side fins, and resemble eels in shape. Hagfish have fleshy "feelers" around the mouth, no eyes, and are also eel-shaped. Both these types feed mainly on other fish, alive or dead.

Lamprey (main) and hagfish (inset)

MAIN GROUPS OF FISH

There are three main groups of fish. The smallest is the jawless type, mainly including types of lampreys and hagfish. They number about 90 species and have rounded mouths with no jawbones but several sharp "teeth." A second group includes sharks, skates, rays, and the deep-sea ratfish. These fish don't have bony skeletons. Their skeletons are made of the bendy, gristly substance called cartilage—the same substance that makes up the tips of our ears and noses. Known as cartilaginous fish, about 800 species make up this group. The third group, bony fish, includes all other fish—almost 30,000 species. They have skeletons made of bone instead of cartilage.

TWO SPEEDS OF BONY FISH

Fish with bony skeletons, like ours, are by far the largest group. They vary from the sleek, speedy barracuda (below) to the S-shaped seahorses (inset), which, at 0.01 miles (0.02 kilometers) per hour, are some of the slowest swimmers.

INSIDE A FISH

A typical fish has fins, scales, and a tail. Inside are most of the main animal organs, or body parts, including the brain, heart, and stomach.

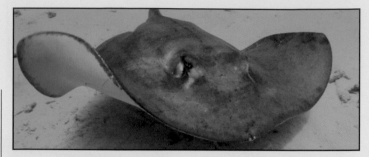

NO SWIM BLADDER
Cartilaginous fish (sharks and rays) do not have swim bladders like bony skeleton fish.

SKELETON
The individual bones of the backbone are known as vertebrae. Pairs of ribs extend up and down from the backbone, strengthening and supporting the body.

Second dorsal fin

Caudal fin (tail)

BACKBONE
Fish belong to the major animal group called the vertebrates. This means the skeleton is based on a row of bones called the vertebral column, or backbone. (However, in sharks, the "backbone" is made of cartilage.) Other vertebrates include reptiles, amphibians, birds, and mammals.

At the front of the vertebral column is the skull, which surrounds and protects the brain. The most obvious features on the outside of the fish's body are the scales and fins.

Anal fin

FINS
The pectorals are the paired fins towards the front, and the pelvics are lower down and further back. Unpaired fins are the dorsal, anal, and caudal, or tail. Different types of fish have varying numbers of fins.

SKELETON AND SWIMMING

The backbone works as a flexible rod along the middle of the body. On each side are blocks of muscle. The muscles on one side bend the bone one way. Then those on the other side flex it the other way.

The bendy backbone allows the fish to swim by making S-shaped curves that swish its tail from side to side.

SWIM BLADDER

The soft, spongy swim bladder is partly filled with gas or air. The amount of gas can be adjusted to make the fish lighter or heavier. This allows the fish to alter its buoyancy and rise, sink, or "hover" in midwater without the effort of swimming.

SCALES

Most bony fish have thin, lightweight scales made of bone. Sharks and rays are covered with tiny tooth-shaped scales called denticles.

Bony fish scales

Shark scales

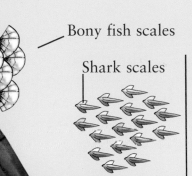

Cerebellum

Optic lobe

Cerebrum

Brain stem

Olfactory lobe

BRAIN

Brain parts include the optic lobes, which deal with vision; the olfactory lobes, which receive information about smell; and the cerebellum, which coordinates muscle movements.

First dorsal fin

Kidney

Liver

Pelvic fin

Pectoral fin

GILLS

Fish breathe through gills instead of lungs. The feathery gills take in oxygen from the water. Their large surface area allows the fish to take in the maximum amount of oxygen.

BREEDING

Most female fish release eggs into the water. The eggs are made in ovaries or "hard roes" and pass along an oviduct, or tube, to the outside. Some kinds of sharks do not lay eggs but give birth to young.

STOMACH AND INTESTINES

A fish passes food from its mouth into its gullet. From there, it goes to the stomach, where it is digested into a mushy soup. The mush oozes along the coiled intestine and nutrients are released. Wastes are removed through the lower rear opening.

HEART

A fish's heart has two main chambers. Used blood from the body flows from the veins into the auricle and on to the ventricle. Here, it is pumped to the gills for fresh oxygen, then around the body and back to the auricle.

Blood to gills and then body

Ventricle

Blood from body

Auricle

FISH THROUGH THE AGES

Cladoselache

Cheirolepis

The first fish appeared in the seas more than 500 million years ago. They looked very different from the fish we know today.

TYPES OF EARLY FISH

Those first fish were agnathans, which means "jawless." They had slitlike mouths and no true fins or scales. By the Devonian Period, from 410 to 355 million years ago, some species had developed biting jaws. One such group was called placoderms, or "plated skins," because of the shieldlike plates of bone that covered their bodies.

During the Devonian Period, or age of fish, sharks also appeared looking very similar to the sharks we know today.

FISH FOSSILS

We know about early fish from their fossils. These are bodies or body parts preserved in rocks and turned to stone. Usually only the hard parts formed fossils, like the bones of this gyrouchus.

PREHISTORIC PREDATORS

These fish lived in the sea about 460 million years ago. The biggest was dunkleosteus, *at more than 16.5 feet (5 m) long. Its "teeth" were sharp bony blades.* Cladoselache *was an early type of shark, 6.6 feet (2 m) in length. The 10-inch (25 centimeters)* cheirolepis *had scales and fins similar to those of modern fish.*

DURING THE AGE OF FISH

Another group of Devonian fish was the acanthodians or "spiny sharks." They were not real sharks but resembled them in shape, and their fins had sharp thorny spines. They died out about 250 million years ago. Several other fish groups have come and gone as well.

Bony fish first appeared 400 million years ago as two main groups. The ray fins (actinopterygians) had fanlike rods supporting their fins, like most fish today. The lobe-fin fish (sarcopterygians) had fins with round, muscular parts at the base. They include the coelacanth (right).

Dunkleosteus

LAST MEAL

Sometimes fish died and were preserved very rapidly, buried by mud or silt on the seabed. Their fossils often show them in the middle of an action. This Mioplosus labracoides was preserved eating its final meal, so we know it was a predator.

FROM FINS TO LIMBS

The only surviving lobe-fin fish is the coelacanth. In ancient times, lobe fins were far more common. One group of lobe fins was the fan sails (rhipidistians). Before they died out, some of them developed their fins into limbs. They became the first land vertebrates, tetrapods, which gave rise to amphibians, reptiles, birds, and mammals.

The coelacanth, once believed to have died out 70 million years ago, was rediscovered in 1938.

FINS, TAILS, AND SWIMMING

Some fish have no fins. Others have large colorful fins to attract mates or even poisonous spines to protect themselves from predators.

SPEED AND CONTROL

Most fish use their fins mainly for swimming. The caudal fin, or tail, swishes from side to side to provide the main forward force. Unpaired fins on the back and underside keep the fish from tilting or rolling over. The paired fins on the sides of the body are for steering and slowing down. Some fish that live in sheltered habitats, such as coral reefs, swim mainly by "rowing" with their side fins.

FLEXIBLE OR STIFF

Bony fish like the smallmouth bass (top) have flexible, movable fins. Cartilaginous fish such as this black-tip reef shark (above) have thick, stiff fins and change direction less easily.

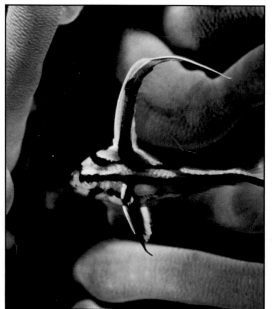

HARD TO RECOGNIZE

The jackknife fish's stripes and long, thin fins break up its body outline. This is known as disruptive coloration.

UNDERWATER SPRINTER

The fastest fish live in the open ocean and have narrow tails, shaped like a V or C. They fold their fins against their body to go at full speed. One of the quickest is the sailfish. It can move at 62 miles (100 km) per hour over short distances, about the same speed as the cheetah on land.

WING FINS

The flying gurnard uses its large pectoral fins for gliding in water as well as for leaping above the surface. Flying fish also have big, winglike fins and glide even farther, sometimes for more than 110 yards (100 m).

FIN RAYS AND MUSCLES

A typical bony fish has fins supported by rodlike spines called fin rays or lepidotrichia. The main surface of the fin is a membrane, or flexible sheet, like thin skin. Body muscles at the base of the fin move the rays so that they can open or close the fin like a fan, or even twist it.

In bony fish, the backbone does not extend into the tail, but in sharks, it goes up into the upper portion of the tail.

STRANGE SHAPE

The ocean sunfish is the biggest bony fish. It grows to 10 feet (3 m) long and can weigh 2 tons (1.8 metric tons). Its dorsal and anal fins are at the rear of the body, and its tail is just a small frill. This fish often lies on its side at the surface, as if sunbathing.

WALKING FISH

Several types of fish have fins on fleshy, armlike "stalks." They work like limbs to push the fish along. Batfish crawl among rocks and seaweed in this way.

The batfish often "walks" along the seabed.

GILLS AND BREATHING

All animals need a constant supply of oxygen. This gas, which makes up one-fifth of the air we breathe, is also found in water.

THE NEED FOR OXYGEN

Oxygen plays a vital part in the chemical processes inside all animals, including humans. Animals breathe oxygen, which is necessary for releasing the energy they need for all life activities. Fish get their oxygen through their gills.

A fish's gills take in about three-quarters of the oxygen from the water flowing past them. (Our own lungs take in only one-quarter of the oxygen in air.) The delicate, feathery gills have a large surface area and a very thin covering so oxygen can pass easily through to the blood inside.

GILL RAKERS

Some fish, like the grouper (above), need gills with small spines or brushlike edges. These gill rakers catch or filter small food items from the water.

GILL SLITS

Oxygen-rich water flows in through a fish's mouth, over the gills, and out through gill slits on the sides of the head. Most sharks must swim to keep the water flowing. Others, like the nurse shark (right), can "pump" it over the gills using mouth muscles. This lets the fish breathe even when still.

In bony fish like this huge arapaima, the gills are covered by a stiff flap. Movement of this flap causes water to swish over the gills. The arapaima lives in South American swamps and "gulps" for air (see below).

MUDSKIPPER

The mudskipper holds water in its large gill chambers. This is so its gills can keep working even above the surface. The mudskipper has to occasionally dip into a pool to refresh this water.

ANOTHER WAY TO BREATHE

Still water contains less oxygen than moving water, and warm water has less oxygen than cold water. So in tropical places, the warm, still water in lakes and swamps is very low in oxygen. In the dry season, fish in these habitats may gradually suffocate from a lack of oxygen as the water dries up.

Some tropical fish come to the surface and gulp air in to their mouth, which then goes into the intestine or swim bladder. From there, oxygen passes through a thin lining into the blood as an extra way of "breathing."

LUNGFISH

Six kinds of eel-shaped lungfish live in tropical swamps in South America, Africa, and Australia. In these fish, the specialized swim bladder has a lining rich in blood vessels (right). The fish swims up to the surface and swallows air into the swim bladder, which works like a lung to pass oxygen from the air into the blood.

A lungfish "breathing" in very shallow water

17

SKIN, SCALES, AND COLOR

Nearly all fish have a protective covering of scales. In some fish these are tiny and lightweight. In others they are heavy "shields" of bone.

SCALES

Most cartilaginous fish, like sharks and rays, have a covering of scales called denticles (placoid scales). They are shaped like tiny teeth. In fact, the real teeth in a shark's mouth are larger versions of these. These denticle scales make shark skin feel rough like sandpaper.

Most bony fish have small, thin scales made of bone. Each scale is joined into the skin at one end and overlaps the scales around it like tiles on a roof. The scales are usually transparent to let the particular colors of the fish's skin show through.

SCALE SIZES AND SHAPES

Eels like the moray (below, left) have very tiny, almost invisible scales set into leathery skin. The mirror carp (below, center) has large, shiny scales. The sturgeon's few big scales (below, right) are thick and reinforced with bone.

Sharks have tiny toothed scales called denticles.

BRIGHT COLORS

At breeding time certain kinds of blennies ①, basslets ②, and gobies ③ brighten their colors to attract a partner. The queen angelfish's glowing hues ④ warn others away from its patch of reef. Predators may attack the fake "eyes" on the end of the four-eye butterfly fish ⑤, but with a quick tail flick, the fish escapes.

PORCUPINE'S SPINES

The porcupine fish is related to the puffer-fish family. Usually its sharp spines are flat (inset). If an enemy comes near, it defends itself by gulping in water. Its body then swells, and the spines stick out (below) and it is too big and prickly to eat.

SKIN AND SLIME

Scales grow from a fish's skin. The epidermis, or thin outer layer of skin, is constantly replacing itself. Below it is the thicker dermis, which contains nerves, blood vessels, and tough, stringlike fibers for strength.

Tiny glands in the skin make a thick, slippery fluid called mucus. It helps to protect the fish against germs, parasites, and the bites of predators. Also, as the fish swims, tiny drops of mucus slip off its body. This helps the fish "slide" through the water more easily.

19

FISHY SENSES

Fish mainly have the same senses that we have—sight, smell, taste, touch, and a form of "hearing." But these all work differently under the water.

SMELL, TASTE, AND ELECTRICITY

A fish uses smell and taste to detect substances in the water. Smell detects from a distance, and taste is used for substances that are close by. Fish taste through tiny taste buds. In some fish, these are inside the mouth, on the outside of the head, and even along the body.

Some fish have the ability to detect electricity. As they move, the muscles of living things give off very small electric pulses that travel well through water. Sharks and some other types of fish use their electric sense to pick up these pulses and detect prey.

"LIVING TONGUE"

Catfish have so many tiny taste buds (sensors) all over the body that they are like "living tongues." In addition, most catfish have fleshy "whiskers" called barbels around the mouth and chin. The barbels are also covered with taste and touch detectors. The catfish uses these to stroke the river or lake bottom to find food.

EEL NOSTRILS

A fish does not use its nostrils for breathing but does use them for smell. Each nostril is a tiny pit or tube, as with this moray (left), lined with microscopic sensors that respond to scent. Some fish, like sharks, can detect the scent of blood from many miles away.

HEARING, BALANCE, AND LATERAL LINES

Fish have simple ears—fluid-filled chambers found under the skin on either side of the head. The ears detect sound vibrations in the water. They also help a fish keep its balance by detecting surrounding movements and the pull of gravity. (This also happens in our own inner ears.) In some fish the ears are linked to the swim bladder, which helps them to pick up even more vibrations. Fish also have lateral lines, or "stripes" along each side of the body. This is a groove or a tube just under the skin with many tiny sensors that respond to ripples and currents in the water. Using its lateral lines, a fish can detect animals moving nearby.

The lateral line arches up and down along the side of this nurse shark's body.

FOUR EYES?

The four-eyed fish has only two eyes, but each has two parts—one to see clearly in air and the other in water. This fish can watch for prey such as insects above and small fish below.

EYES AND SIGHT

Inside, fish eyes are similar to our own. However, most fish have eyes on the sides of their heads. This lets them see almost all around them. Also, the deeper the water gets, the more the eye absorbs color, especially reds. So fish probably see colors very differently from the way we do.

Most fish that live near the surface have large eyes and can see well. Fish in deeper waters have even bigger eyes to see in the gloom. However, below a depth of 0.62 miles (1 km), there is no light. Many deep-sea fish have tiny, almost useless eyes and are black like their surroundings.

HOW FISH BREED

E ach fish is either male or
female, and one of each is
needed to produce young. Some fish
live and breed in huge shoals with
thousands of other fish.

COURTSHIP
Like many animals, fish carry out
behavior called courtship before they
breed. This often includes displaying
colorful parts of the body and actions
such as swimming in a zigzag manner,
waving fins, and rubbing, touching, or
even biting their partner.

Courtship allows each fish to check
that a possible partner is of the same
species, is of the opposite sex, and is
healthy and suitable for breeding.

THE STORY OF THE SALMON
*After a few years in the sea, salmon swim
upriver ①, back to the stream where they
hatched. They have to swim against powerful
currents. Females and males then breed ②,
and the small eggs are laid in the gravel on the
streambed ③ The eggs hatch as tiny babies
called alevins, which feed on the egg yolk ④.
They then grow into young fish called parr ⑤.
About two to four years after hatching, they
become young salmon, or smolts, ⑥ and swim
downriver to the sea.*

COLORFUL COURTING
*This courting male stickleback has developed a red
underside to attract the female. He also builds a simple
nest where she will lay her eggs.*

SPAWNING
In most species, the female releases eggs,
or roe, into the water. The male stays very
near and releases his sperm, or milt. The
sperm then fertilize, or join with, the eggs,
and the baby fish start to grow. In some
species, many males and females do this
together as part of a large breeding shoal.

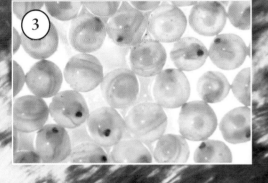

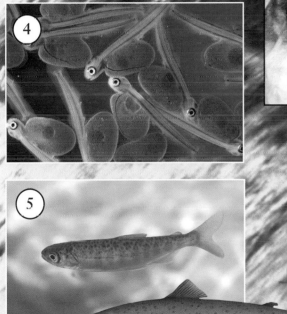

PUPS OR EGGS

Some sharks give birth to babies called pups (left). Others lay hard-cased eggs, or "mermaid's purses" (inset).

SAFE MOUTH

Mouthbreeders keep their eggs in their mouths. When the babies hatch they swim nearby, but can dash back to the parent's mouth for safety.

SPLASHING TETRA

The splashing tetra female leaps above the water to lay her eggs on overhanging leaves. Above the water, the eggs are safe from other fish. To keep them from drying out, the male must then splash them until the eggs hatch and the young drop in the water.

Splashing tetras keep their eggs wet.

GIVING BIRTH

Certain fish do not lay eggs. The male passes his sperm into the female's body and fertilization takes place there. The eggs then develop inside the female, and she gives birth to the babies. Several sharks, including the giant whale shark, breed in this way.

THE SHARK GROUP

There are about 330 different species of shark, and this includes the biggest type of fish. All are carnivores, or meat-eaters.

GREAT HUNTERS

The biggest hunting fish is the great white. As with many fish, its size is sometimes exaggerated in "fish tales." In reality, it is 6.5 to 7.5 yards (6 to 7 m) long and weighs up to 2 tons (1.8 metric tons). Great whites prefer warm-blooded victims such as seals, sea lions, dolphins, and even humans.

Several other big predatory sharks are dangerous to people, including the tiger shark, hammerhead, and bull shark. The bull shark, or river whaler, is one of the few fish that can swim from the sea into rivers. It has attacked people in lakes thousands of miles from the sea.

THE GREATEST HUNTER
The great white, or white pointer, charges prey at great speeds and delivers a massive bite. It waits until the victim weakens and then eats it.

STREAMLINED KILLER
The 4.5 yard (4 m) long blue shark is found in more seas and oceans than any other fish.

DEADLY TAIL

The thresher shark's leathery, straplike tail (left) can be longer than the rest of its body. The shark thrashes its tail at a shoal of smaller fish, stunning them and making them easier to catch.

RISING AND DIVING

Unlike bony fish, sharks do not have the body part called the swim bladder. They cannot change their buoyancy to rise or dive in the water. However, a shark does have a different buoyancy aid. This is its large liver, which is rich in oily fluids. Oil is lighter than water, so the liver helps the shark stay high in the water. But the liver's buoyancy cannot be adjusted. So most sharks must actively swim to dive deep. In a big shark, the liver can be a quarter of its total body weight.

JAWS AND TEETH

A typical shark's teeth are very sharp and slim like blades. They often snap off if the shark struggles with prey. However, new teeth growing on the inside of the jaw are always ready to replace them. The spare teeth gradually move into useful positions. A shark can go through thousands of teeth during its lifetime.

New teeth grow on the inside of the jaw.

Older teeth break off when feeding.

BIGGEST FISH

A whale shark cruising slowly

The whale shark is the largest fish in the world. It reaches 14.3 yards (13 m) long and more than 15 (13.5 metric tons) tons in weight. This giant fish is not an active hunter. Using its gill rakers, it filters tiny creatures called plankton from the water.

"SNAKES OF THE SEA"

Eels are sometimes called snakes of the sea. They are not snakes, which are reptiles, but long, slim fish. More than 600 kinds live around the world.

STRANGE-SHAPED CAVE DWELLERS

A typical eel has a very long dorsal fin along its back and a similar anal fin on its underside; the two fins join together around the tail end. Eeels also have pectoral side fins, but no pelvic fins. An eel may have more than 100 vertebrae, or backbones, which let it bend, curl, and even tie its body in a knot.

Most eels, such as morays and congers, live in the sea. They often lurk in caves or rocks and watch for passing prey. Divers are advised not to poke or prod into rock cracks and crevices. A bite from an eel is painful and can become infected.

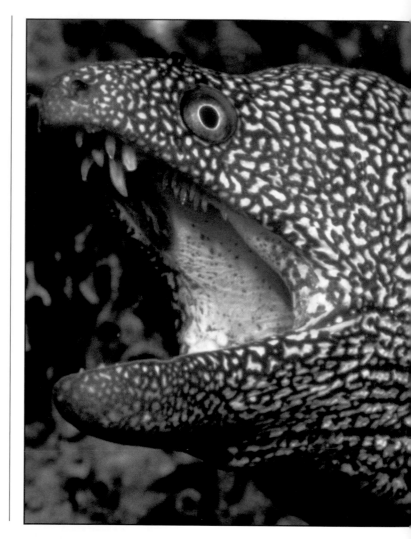

"GARDEN" OF EELS

Garden eels live in groups and look like plants growing on the seabed. When feeding, each eel keeps its tail in its burrow in the sand or mud. Its upper body sways in the current to grab small food like young fish. At the first hint of danger, these eels shoot down into their burrows, and the "garden" disappears.

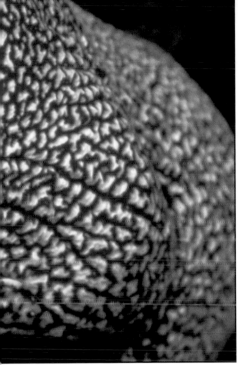

MORAY EELS

The moray family contains about 100 species, like the spotted moray (left) and leopard moray (above). All are hunters and catch a variety of prey, from fish and crabs to octopus. Most are protective of their territories, or areas where they live, chasing away other eels that come too close.

LONGEST, SLIMMEST

The largest eels, like the Australian long-tailed reef eel, reach more than 13 feet (4 m) in length. Snake eels (above) are among the slimmest and can be thinner than a pencil.

TRAVELING TO BREED

Several kinds of freshwater eels leave lakes and rivers in Europe and North America and swim to the Sargasso Sea, in the West Atlantic Ocean, to breed. Their eggs hatch into tiny, leaf-shaped larvae, or young. These then head back home. They change shape and swim up rivers as small, see-through glass eels. Then they grow into yellowish young called elvers.

FISH WITH A SHOCK

The electric eel is not actually an eel but a member of the catfish group. It lives in tropical rivers and swamps in South America. Large blocks of muscles along its body have evolved to produce electricity, which passes into the water. The fish can detect when nearby objects interfere with the electric pulses, and this helps it to find its way in cloudy muddy water. Powerful jolts can also be made to stun prey or deter enemies.

The electric eel can reach 8 feet (2.4 m) in length.

CATFISH, COD, AND ANGLERFISH

Three of the most fascinating groups of fish are also important as food for humans. They are eaten all over the world.

CATFISH

There are more than 2,000 species of catfish. Most live in fresh water and are bottom-feeders. They nose in the mud for worms, shellfish, and any edible bits and pieces, using their sensitive, whiskerlike barbels to detect food.

Catfish range in size from the transparent glass catfish of Africa, at just 4 inches (10 cm) long, to giants measuring more than 10 feet (3 m) in length. These huge catfish include the wels of Europe, which can swallow a duck, and the Mekong catfish of Southeast Asia, which can weigh 550 pounds (250 kilograms) or more.

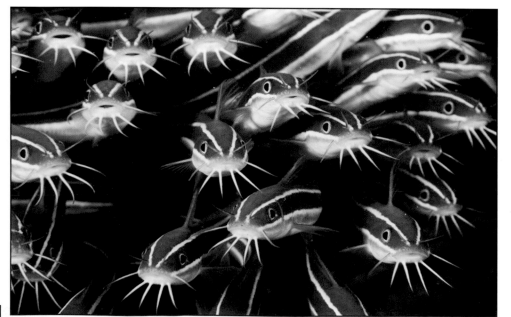

TWO KINDS OF CATFISH

The brown or green catfish, also known as the bullhead (above), has jagged spines. It has venom glands that protect it from predators. Barber-eel catfish (left) gather in shoals for safety. Catfish lack true scales, but some have bony skin plates for protection.

ATLANTIC COD

Some cod once grew to more than 3.3 feet (1 m) long and 198 pounds (90 kg) in weight. But overfishing by people means most are killed before they reach their full size.

COD AND THEIR COUSINS

The cod group includes more than 600 species such as haddock, hake, pollock, whiting, and grenadiers. (These are also related to anglerfish.) Nearly all live in the sea, and many are caught for food. The Atlantic cod feeds on smaller fish and forms huge shoals. Each female releases more than 5 million eggs, which drift in the water and provide important food for many smaller kinds of fish and sea life.

The sargassum fish is a type of frogfish that lives among huge floating mats of sargassum seaweed, found in warmer oceans. It is very well-camouflaged. Its skin has flaps, frills and tassels, and is colored to match the weeds around it. Like the batfish, it has armlike fins and can crawl well along the seabed.

A sargassum fish tries to hide among weeds.

ANGLERFISH

There are more than 200 species of anglerfish, frogfish, batfish, and goosefish. Many have a fin spine on the head tipped with a fleshy "bait" to attract prey, which the angler then gulps into its big mouth.

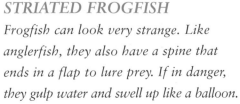

FRILLED ANGLER

This anglerfish is almost impossible to see as it lies in wait among weeds and rocks. It uses its fin spine like a fishing rod to lure prey.

STRIATED FROGFISH

Frogfish can look very strange. Like anglerfish, they also have a spine that ends in a flap to lure prey. If in danger, they gulp water and swell up like a balloon.

GRENADIER

Also called a rat tail, this deep-sea fish's tail goes into a point. This member of the cod group makes a drumming sound when it breeds.

FLATTENED FISH

Two very different groups of fish have flat bodies. One group includes rays and skates; the flatfish group includes plaice, sole, and flounders.

RAYS' BODIES

Rays are cartilaginous fish and are related to sharks. A ray's body is flattened from top to bottom, so it can lie on the seabed on its underside. The pectoral fins are extended into wide wings, which the ray flaps to "fly" through the water.

DIFFERENT DEFENSES

The blue-spotted stingray (inset) has a daggerlike spine along its tail. It uses this to jab its enemies with poison. The giant manta or "devil fish" (bottom) relies on size and power for defense.

RAY AND SKATE FACTS

There are about 450 species of rays and skates. Rays are more common in tropical seas, while skates are found in cooler northern and southern waters. Nearly all kinds are predators. Most search along the seabed for worms, shellfish, and other prey, crunching them up with strong, flattened teeth. When resting, a ray flaps sand or mud over itself to hide.

HIGH-VOLTAGE RAY

Electric rays have specialized muscles that can give out powerful shocks of more than 200 volts.

A marbled ray is one of several electric rays.

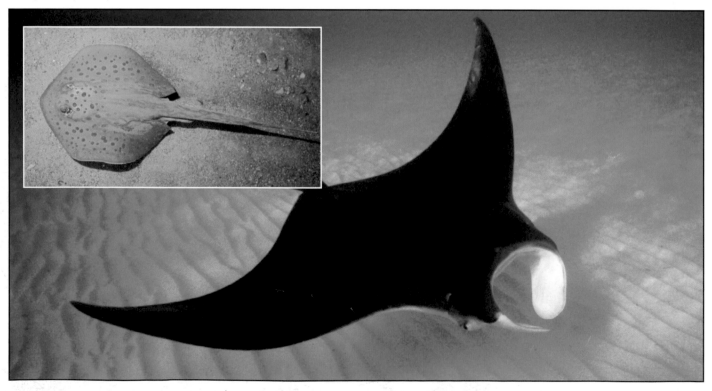

SIDEWAYS LOOKER

The peacock flounder (below and main) lies on its right side. It is a "left-eye" flatfish because both eyes are on its left side, allowing it to look upward. This flounder grows to about 20 inches (50 cm) in length. Many flatfish can change skin color to blend in against the ocean floor.

FLATFISH

Like rays, flatfish live on the seabed. But unlike rays, they are bony fish and are flattened from side to side instead of from top to bottom. So a flatfish lies on either its left or right side, depending on the species. In a normal fish, this would mean one eye looking down. However, in a flatfish, one eye moves across the head during early growth. As an adult flatfish, both eyes are located on one side of the body.

There are about 500 types of flatfish, and many are caught for food by humans. Among the largest are the halibuts, at more than 6.5 feet (2 m) long and weighing more than 660 pounds (300 kg).

FISH OF LAKES AND RIVERS

Around the world, fish are the main inhabitants of streams, rivers, ponds, and lakes. Some are peaceful plant-eaters; others are powerful predators.

FRESHWATER CONDITIONS

Fish are cold-blooded, so their body temperatures vary with their surroundings. In northern and southern regions, freshwater fish become inactive during cold winters. They hardly move and need little or no food. Even if ice forms on the surface, they can usually survive below by burying themselves in mud.

Some freshwater fish are suited to fast-flowing streams. These strong swimmers are able to resist being swept along by the current, often just by hiding behind rocks or weeds. Others are more suited to slow rivers and still lakes.

CARP

The carp family is the biggest of all fish families, with more than 1,500 species found in most freshwater habitats. Certain types of carp are detritivores. This means they feed on detritus—a mix of tiny plants, animals, and old, decaying matter found on the river or lake bed. In this way they take in valuable nutrients that might otherwise be wasted.

COLORFUL CARP

Many kinds of carp have been bred for their colors, like grass carp from Asia (right) and more familiar types such as goldfish (inset).

WALLEYES

The walleye has a reflective layer over its eyes, just like in a cat's eyes. The layer causes the eyes to glow and helps the fish to see at night.

RIVERS AND LAKES

The rainbow trout (main) needs fast-flowing river water with plenty of oxygen. Lake trout, such as the charr (inset), can survive in still waters with less oxygen.

PIRANHA

Red piranhas (right) often eat fruits, seeds, and small creatures. But in a shoal, their razor-sharp teeth can strip flesh from a large animal in minutes.

YELLOW PERCH

The vertical stripes on these fish camouflage them among waterweeds, allowing them to catch prey by surprise.

PIKE

The pike is a sleek hunter found in lakes and quiet rivers in northern regions. Up to 4.5 feet (1.4 m) long, it lurks in plants and dashes out to grab prey in its wide mouth.

SHOOTING AT PREY

Archerfish live in streams and rivers in Southeast Asia and can also survive in the somewhat salty waters found in river mouths and other places where rivers meet seas. The fish are called archerfish because they hunt their prey by squirting "arrows" of water from their mouths into the air above. (An archer is a person who uses a bow and arrow.) These water jets stun insects and other small prey that live above the water.

An archerfish aims its jetlike blast of water.

SEASHORE FISH

The seashore may seem a pleasant place for us to visit, but it is not so for most fish. This is because it exposes them to many risks and dangers.

A CHANGING HABITAT

Seashore fish live in a changing habitat. On sunny days, the water in sheltered pools can get very hot and salty, but on rainy days, floods of fresh water can dilute the salt. On windy days, storms can cause huge waves to crash on the coast, hurling pebbles and rocks. All this means that the fish that live there must be tough, with fast reactions.

GOBIES GALORE

Hundreds of types of gobies wriggle along shores around the world. Many, like this common goby, have pelvic fins on the underside that create suction to hold the fish firmly on to rocks.

PIPES, TRUMPETS, AND DRAGONS

Pipefish ① and trumpetfish ② have small mouths and eat tiny plants and animals. They are difficult to see among seaweed stems. Their close relative, the weedy seadragon ③, is a type of seahorse that feeds in the same way.

FROM FEMALE TO MALE

Ballan wrasse are all born as females and are ready to breed at about five or six years old. After a few more years, some of them change sex and become male. There are no outward signs of this. Females and males look much the same and are usually green.

When a dominant male wrasse dies, the nearest senior female changes sex and takes his place as "top" male.

ZONES ALONG THE SHORELINE

The toughest fish, like blennies and gobies, live in shallow parts of the shore. Many can survive out of water for short amounts of time if trapped by rocks when the tide goes out. The deep shore offers additional safety because it is covered by water for longer periods of time at each tide. Seaweed also provides shelter from sunshine, drying winds, and surging waves.

The tides, winds, and waves provide benefits, too. They wash onto the shore all kinds of animals and plants that provide food for shoreline fish.

HIDDEN DANGER

In Southeast Asia and northern Australia the lumpy, mottled stonefish is hard to spot in the rocky shallows along the shores. But its poisonous fin spines can kill a person.

SAWFISH

This huge fish, which grows up to 6.6 yards (6 m), is a type of ray. It prefers shallow coastal waters and uses its "chain-saw" snout to stir up mud and small prey like worms. It will also use the snout to swipe at small fish passing by.

THE COLORFUL REEF

Coral reefs are the tropical forests of the underwater world, containing more fish and sea creatures than any other aquatic habitat.

WHY SO BRIGHT?

Few animals are as brightly colored as tropical fish. Their patterns have many meanings. Some colors are needed so that fish can recognize others of their own species for breeding. They show whether a fish is male or female and old enough to breed. Other fish use their coloration to warn intruders away from their territories or to show that they taste horrible and should not be attacked. Colors and patterns also camouflage fish and sea creatures against the coral.

BEWARE MY VENOM!

The long, striped spines and bright shades of the lionfish, or scorpionfish, are there to warn intruders away. The poisonous spines are strong enough to kill humans.

Lionfish (Indian and West Pacific Oceans)

DAZZLING PATTERNS

The edge of a coral reef is filled with fish of every imaginable color and pattern. See above: black-tip reef shark ①; great barracuda ②; sergeant-major fish ③; parrot fish ④; a variety of wrasses ⑤; giant grouper ⑥; puffer fish ⑦; blue-backed wrasse ⑧; queen triggerfish ⑨; exquisite butterfly fish ⑩; Bennett's butterfly fish ⑪; regal angelfish ⑫; latticed butterfly fish ⑬; clown triggerfish ⑭; young yellow boxfish ⑮; and queen angelfish ⑯.

DYING AND LIVING TOGETHER

Battles of life and death occur daily on the reef, as predators hunt for food. At the same time, some species help each other survive. This is called symbiosis. For example, clown fish live near the tentacles of sea anemones, where they are safe from predators. In return, the fish is "bait" to lure other creatures, which the anemone then captures.

Clown fish stay near their anemone partners.

OPEN OCEAN DWELLERS

Seas and oceans are the largest habitats, covering more than two-thirds of Earth. The biggest, fastest, and most spectacular fish live here.

FOOD CHAINS
Tiny drifting plants and animals called plankton are at the bottom of the ocean's food chain. The plankton is food for small creatures like young fish. In turn, these are eaten by larger fish, and so on, along the different food chains. At the top of the chains are huge predatory fish such as sharks and marlins.

FAST LEAPERS
Dolphinfish can leap above the surface like their mammal namesakes, real dolphins.

FEEDING TOGETHER
Tuna (below) have the curved fins and narrow C-shaped tail of fast swimmers. The largest types, like the yellowfin, are 6.6 feet (2 m) in length. They form big shoals that feed on even larger shoals of smaller fish, such as anchovies (inset).

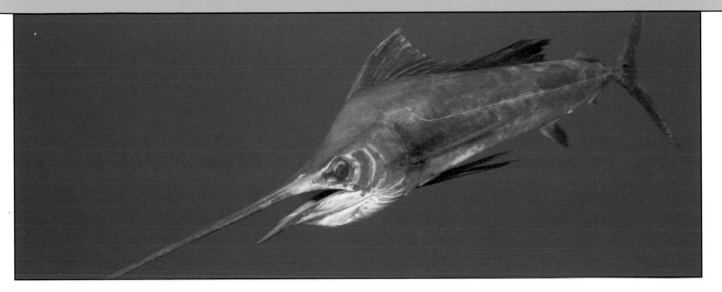

COLOR AND SHADE

The open ocean has no seaweeds or rocks where camouflaged fish can hide from enemies. So many ocean fish have countershading—a darker back and lighter underside. Seen from above, the dark back merges with the gloom of the depths below. Viewed from beneath, the pale underside blends with the lightness of the water's surface.

BLUE FROM ABOVE

The blue marlin is dark blue on top but silvery white underneath. This hides it from its prey.

SHOALS

Many smaller fish like mackerel, herrings, and anchovies form large close-knit shoals, or groups, that move together like one giant creature. This may confuse predators who try to single out one victim.

BIGGEST EATS SMALLEST

At 11 yards (10 m), the basking shark is the world's second-largest fish, after the whale shark. Like its massive cousin, it filters tiny items of food from the plankton, using its brushlike gill rakers.

LEAP TO FREEDOM

Flying fish have large side fins that work like wings to glide above the surface. They gain speed underwater, then they leap clear of the surface. This is usually to escape predators.

A flying fish in action

A t about 550 yards (500 m) below the ocean's surface, there is no light at all. In this immense, constant blackness live some of the strangest fish of all.

NO LIGHT TO SEE

Many deep-sea fish are very dark or black and have tiny or no eyes. This is because without light, there is no purpose in being colorful or camouflaged or seeing well. No plants can grow in the darkness so deep-sea fish either feed on the "rain" of food sinking slowly from above, such as the dead bodies of fish and other creatures, or they try to hunt each other.

With limited food in such a vast realm, most deep-sea fish are small, less than 20 inches (50 cm) long. One of the deepest-living is the abyssal cusk eel, which is just 8 inches (20 cm) long. It has been detected more than 0.5 miles (0.8 km) below the West Atlantic Ocean's surface.

GLOWING "BAIT"

Like its shallow-water cousins, the deep-sea anglerfish uses a fleshy tipped fin spine as a "fishing rod." The tip glows to tempt prey.

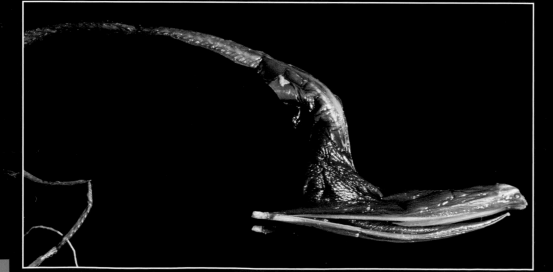

A BIG GULP

In the deep, it is wise to grab food if it comes near. The gulper, or pelican eel, has very wide jaws and a stretchy mouth that can fit prey far larger than itself. This eel is about 28 inches (70 cm) long and has a glowing tip to its tail that attracts prey.

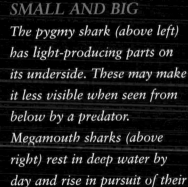

SMALL AND BIG

The pygmy shark (above left) has light-producing parts on its underside. These may make it less visible when seen from below by a predator. Megamouth sharks (above right) rest in deep water by day and rise in pursuit of their plankton food at night.

DEEPWATER SHARKS

The smallest sharks include the pygmy shark at only 10 inches (25 cm) in length. It has a spine on its dorsal fin, probably to deter predators from biting it. Much larger, and also more mysterious, is the megamouth. Since it was discovered in 1976, only about 25 have been recorded. It grows to 6.6 yards (6 m) long. Like the whale and basking sharks, it swims with its huge mouth open to filter small food.

LIVING LIGHT

Here and there in the dark depths are eerie glowing spots and patches. They are made by light-producing parts called photophores found on the bodies of certain fish. This is a process known as bioluminescence. Some fish have lights in rows or patterns, so they can recognize their own species for breeding. Others use their lights as "bait" to lure and catch their prey. More than 1,500 kinds of fish are bioluminescent.

A flashlight fish's patches shine on and off.

FISH IN TROUBLE

On land, we can see nature being destroyed, and the animals put at risk. In the water, these threats are less visible, but they are just as real.

SCALE OF THE PROBLEM

The official lists of threatened animals show that about one fish species in every 30 is at risk. But these numbers come from a very limited number of species that have been properly studied. In reality, it is thought that almost one species in two is threatened.

Fish face many of the same problems as animals on land. One of the main threats is habitat destruction. The natural homes of fish and other water life have gradually been taken over by humans and been used to build ports, power stations, oil refineries, and water parks.

DYNAMITE DESTRUCTION

Explosives used to kill and catch large numbers of fish at once also destroy every scrap of life in the area. Some habitats will never recover.

OVERFISHING

Seafood dishes like fish and chips or soup made with sharks' fins (left) have a long history, and many people make a living from fishing (inset). But as more fish are caught, their numbers decrease. If numbers fall too low, the species may never recover. An additional problem is that many fish are caught and injured by accident and thrown back.

FISH FARMS

Salmon are raised in large cages at sea, while captive trout and carp are grown in freshwater streams and ponds. This helps to reduce fish catches from the wild.

POLLUTION

Fish are killed by harmful chemicals in a river—an obvious case of pollution. But even greater damage happens unseen, in remote areas and out at sea.

SPREADING MENACE

Another serious threat is pollution. Dangerous chemicals pour from shore-side factories and flow into the sea from rivers, damaging water life over huge areas.

Litter is another problem. Fish who are attracted by shiny bits of plastic eat them and soon die. One of the greatest threats, though, is overfishing. Too many people catch too many fish. If we can reduce mass fishing and lessen the wastes and chemicals we dump into the water, we can start to save fish and water life.

HELPING HANDS

Rare fish like the sturgeon can be caught and "milked" for their eggs or sperm (inset), which are used to breed more young.

ANIMAL CLASSIFICATION

The animal kingdom can be split into two main groups, vertebrates (with a backbone) and invertebrates (without a backbone). From these two main groups, scientists classify, or sort, animals further based on their shared characteristics.

The six main groupings of animals, from the most general to the most specific, are: phylum, class, order, family, genus, and species. This system was created by Carolus Linnaeus.

To see how this system works, follow the example of how human beings are classified in the vertebrate group and how earthworms are classified in the invertebrate group.

ANIMAL KINGDOM

VERTEBRATE	INVERTEBRATE
PHYLUM: Chordata	**PHYLUM:** Annelida
CLASS: Mammals	**CLASS:** Oligochaeta
ORDER: Primates	**ORDER:** Haplotaxida
FAMILY: Hominids	**FAMILY:** Lumbricidae
GENUS: *Homo*	**GENUS:** *Lumbricus*
SPECIES: *sapiens*	**SPECIES:** *terrestris*

ANIMAL PHYLA

There are more than 30 groups of phyla. The nine most common are listed below along with their common name.

Annelida
(SEGMENTED WORMS)

Arthropoda
(ARTHROPODS)

CHORDATA
(CHORDATES)

Cnidaria
(CNIDARIANS)

Echinodermata
(ECHINODERMS)

Mollusca
(MOLLUSKS)

Nematoda
(ROUNDWORMS)

Platyhelminthes
(FLATWORMS)

Porifera
(SPONGES)

This book highlights animals from the Chordata phylum. Follow the example below to learn how scientists classify the *funebris*, or green moray eel.

VERTEBRATE

PHYLUM: Chordata

CLASS: Actinopterygii

ORDER: Anguilliformes

FAMILY: Muraenidae

GENUS: *Gymnothorax*

SPECIES: *funebris*

Green moray eel
(funebris)

GLOSSARY

BARBELS
Fleshy flaps or "whiskers" around the mouth of certain fish, such as catfish, which are sensitive to water currents, touch, smell, and taste

BIOLUMINESCENCE
Production of light by living things so that they glow, shine, or flash in dark surroundings

BONY FISH
A class of fish (Osteichthyes) with a skeleton made of bone; most fish belong to this group, except for sharks, rays, skates, and ratfish (chimaeras)

BUOYANCY
Ability to float

CAMOUFLAGE
The disguising of an animal by the way it is colored and patterned to blend or merge with its surroundings

CARTILAGINOUS FISH
A class of fish (Chondrichthyes) with an inner supporting skeleton made of cartilage ("gristle") instead of bone; the main species in this group are sharks, rays, skates, and ratfish (chimaeras)

COLD-BLOODED
Having a body temperature that varies with the temperature of one's surroundings, so an animal is cool in cold weather and warm in hot sunny weather

COUNTERSHADING
Skin coloring such that an animal's body is dark on its upper side and lighter underneath; seen from below, the animal merges with the sunlight, and from above, it merges with the darkness of the deep water below

DENTICLES
Small toothlike scales on the body of sharks and similar fish, giving their skin a rough texture like sandpaper

DETRITIVORE
An animal that feeds on matter consisting of dead and dying bits and pieces from various larger animals and plants, called detritus

FIN RAYS
Long rods or spines that hold out the flexible fins of ray-finned fish and change the fin's size and shape for swimming; in some fish they are sharp for defense

GILL RAKERS
Projections that look like hairs, brushes, or rakes on the gills of certain fish; they are used in feeding to filter small items of food from the water

HABITAT
A particular type of surroundings or environment where plants and animals live, such as a desert, mountainside, pond, river, seashore, or coral reef

LATERAL LINE
A long, thin sensory part that looks like a stripe or line along each side of a fish's body; it is used to detect ripples and currents in the water

MILT
Liquid containing sperm released by a male fish at breeding time

MUCUS
A slimy substance made by a fish's skin that helps to protect the fish and lets it slide easily through the water

PLANKTON
The mixture of small plants and animals that drift through the water in seas, oceans, and large lakes

ROE
The mass of eggs inside a female fish or just released into the water

SCALES
Small, hard parts that cover the body of fish for protection and streamlined swimming; they are differing sizes and shapes depending on the fish

SHOAL
A large group of fish that swims together

SWIM BLADDER
A spongy or gas-filled part inside a bony fish that can be adjusted to alter the fish's weight and buoyancy; this is so the fish can rise, sink, or stay at the same level in the water with little effort

SYMBIOSIS
Relationships involving two or more very different kinds of animals that live closely together; sometimes both benefit from the relationship

VERTEBRATE
An animal with a backbone and spinal cord; vertebrates include mammals, birds, reptiles, amphibians, and fish

FURTHER RESOURCES

AT THE LIBRARY
Hirschmann, Kris. *Rays*. San Diego: Kidhaven Press, 2003.

Mallory, Kenneth. *Swimming with Hammerhead Sharks*. Boston: Houghton Mifflin, 2001.

Parker, Steve. *Fish*. New York: Dorling Kindersley, 2005.

Walker, Sally M. *Fossil Fish Found Alive: Discovering the Coelacanth*. Minneapolis: Carolrhoda, 2002.

ON THE WEB
For more information on *fish,* use FactHound to track down Web sites related to this book.

1. *Go to www.facthound.com*
2. Type in a search word related to this book or this book ID: 0756512522
3. Click on the *Fetch It* button

FactHound will find the best Web sites for you.

INDEX

A
anchovies, 38, 39
anemones, 37
angelfish, 19, 36
anglerfish, 29, 40
arapaima, 17
archerfish, 33
B
barracuda, 9, 36
basking shark, 39, 41
bass, 14
basslets, 19
batfish, 15, 29
blennies, 19, 35
blue shark, 24
bony fish, 9, 15, 18 25, 31
boxfish, 36
breeding, 11, 14, 19, 22–23, 36, 41
bull shark, 24
bullheads, 28
butterfly fish, 36
C
camouflage, 29, 31, 33, 35, 36, 39
carp, 18, 32, 33,
cartilaginous fish, 9, 10, 14, 18, 30
catfish, 20, 27, 28
char, 33
clown fish, 37
cod, 29
coelacanth, 12, 13
coral reefs, 8, 14, 36–37
cusk eel, 40
D
deep-sea fish, 20,

40–41
dolphinfish, 38
E
eagle ray, 8
eels, 8, 18, 20, 26–27, 40
eggs, 11, 22, 23, 27, 29, 43
electric eel, 27
electric rays, 30
F
fins, 10, 12, 14–15, 26, 30, 39
fishing, 42, 43
flashlight fish, 41
flatfish, 30, 31
flounders, 30, 31
flying fish, 15, 39
fossils, 12, 13
four-eyed fish, 21
freshwater fish, 8, 32–33
frogfish, 29
G
giant grouper, 36
gills, 11, 16–17
glass catfish, 28
gobies, 6, 19, 34, 35
goldfish, 6, 32
goosefish, 29
great white shark, 6, 24, 25
grenadiers, 29
gurnard, 15
H
habitat, 8, 14, 17, 33, 36, 38, 42
haddock, 29
hagfish, 8, 9
hake, 29
halibuts, 31
hammerhead shark, 24

herrings, 39
J
jackknife fish, 14
jawfish, 23
jawless fish, 8, 9, 12
L
lampreys, 8, 9, 12
lateral line, 21
lionfish, 36
lungfish, 13, 17
M
mackerel, 39
manta ray, 30
marlins, 38, 39
megamouth sharks, 41
mouthbreeders, 23
mudskipper, 17
N
nurse shark, 21
P
parrot fish, 36
perch, 33
pike, 33
pipefish, 34
piranhas, 32
plaice, 30
pollock, 29
pollution, 43
porcupine fish, 19
puffer fish, 19, 36
pygmy shark, 41
R
ratfish, 9
rays, 6, 9, 10, 11, 18, 30, 35
reef shark, 8, 14, 36
S
sailfish, 14
salmon, 8, 22, 43
sargassum fish, 29
sawfish, 35

scales, 10, 11, 12, 18–19
scorpionfish, 36
seahorse, 9, 34
sergeant-major fish, 36
sharks, 6, 8, 11, 12, 15, 18, 23, 24–25
  breeding, 22–23
  food chains, 38
  gills, 16
  senses, 20, 21
  skeleton, 9, 10
shore fish, 34–35
skates, 9, 10, 30
sole, 30
spiny shark, 12
stickleback, 22
stingray, 30
stonefish, 35
sturgeon, 18, 43
sunfish, 15
T
tetra, 23
thresher shark, 25
tiger shark, 24
triggerfish, 36
trout, 33, 43
trumpetfish, 34
tuna, 38
W
walleye, 32
weedy seadragon, 34
whale shark, 23, 25, 39, 41
wrasse, 6, 35, 36